# FINDING

# THE AMERICAN

# MALE

## -LOST AND FOUND-

# WRITTEN BY:  ED BREEDING

## COPYRIGHT:  ED BREEDING - 6/1/2020

# PREFACE

As a Two-Spirit person, I have spent a lifetime observing and being acquainted with the average heterosexual American male, and after many years of observation, I have had the privilege of seeing how he has gone from someone who was very comfortable with his male role, to presently finding himself uncomfortable, confused, and uncertain about what it is to be a modern man who is joyful and at peace with himself.

Throughout recorded history the gender role of a man or a woman has been clearly defined, and prior to the advent of automation and the speed of which technology has progressed, there was seldom any need for the man or woman to question their prescribed role in society, but today their roles have been blurred, and many have been left confused and disillusioned as to who they truly are.

Perhaps we have all heard the phrase, "the love of money is the root of all evil," and maybe we have never given the phrase much thought previously, but now if we look at the power and control that mass media and materialistic advertising has over us, all for the lust and love of money, the phrase takes on a very important meaning, and something we can all learn from.

Up until the past century women have, generally speaking, been considered second-class citizens. They had not been considered equal to men in many places of society, and thereby the pressure has not  been so heavy on them to perform in their gender roles as it has been for men. The Judeo-Christian belief system has kept them subjugated to the will of men, until…modern times. And now everything has changed, and rightfully so for the sake of women's freedoms and equal place in society, but as women have suffered, fought and gained their rights of equality, in many cases, the American male has fallen behind and oftentimes questioned his masculinity, whenever he has to come to terms with the fact that a woman is equal to him in every way.

It is this writer's hope that *Finding the American Male* will shed a brighter light on where the American male has been, where he is today, and what lies ahead for him.

# Finding the American Male
# Chapter 1

Europeans first came to these North American shores for religious freedom, land, opportunities for personal betterment, and in general, a better way of life. During the Colonial period the American male was perhaps launched into what would be his most physically demanding role.  In many cases, the early colonists' desire and zeal to achieve what he had not been able to achieve in Europe was not always matched by their physical and mental ability to do so.

The first few winters were known to be especially difficult for the colonists, and many of them did not survive.  Though they planned for their venture in the New World as best they could, they were, nevertheless, ill-prepared for what lay before them. Lack of food and proper shelter were major enemies. After many deaths from these hardships the colonists soon began to learn the art of survival.

A major contributor to the success of the colonists was learning about how to survive from lessons given by the American Indian. From the Indians' assistance, the colonists were beginning to learn how to better live off the land.

It is this writer's belief that if the American male had genuinely adhered to more of the Indians' ways of life in the New World, rather than hold so tenaciously to his European ways, he could possibly have fewer problems today with his male-role-identity, because many of the tribes recognized and accepted up to five gender roles. In retrospect, could we dare imagine that it may have been Creator's plan for his runaway

European children to have left behind more of their habits and ideas from decadent Europe and learn and apply more of what the Indians and the new land had to teach them about the diversity of Creator and a more peaceful way of life?  Rather than constantly changing the landscape to meet their needs, may they not have been better off to change themselves to meet the ways of the land?  Although the Indians maintained territorial boundaries and had warfare, they did not believe that an individual could own the land.  On the contrary, it was their belief that they were part of the land, as were the trees and animals that roamed the forest, and they considered all living things their relations.  And even though the Indian found it necessary to kill animals for food, they also understood the importance of offering up a prayer of thanksgiving to the animal for giving its life, whereby the Indian might live.

At this point one might wonder what those Indian practices had to do with the American male's role-image. Perhaps the key and pivotal word here is 'Respect'; respect for self and others, our Earth Mother, and all living things. Without the respect for others, we lose it for ourselves, and thereby open Pandora's Box for many more problems to follow.

Although the seeds for much of our contemporary American male's problems were brought with the colonists from Europe, they, nevertheless, were probably at their healthiest, so far as a male-role-identity, during the Colonial period. Because it was at that time, more so than any other time in our American history, that the man best knew his male role, as he deemed it to be, and was closest to being one with the land.

Though the hardships were extreme and many for men and women, the survival of the colonists was contingent on how well each played his/her appropriate role.

Looking back on history during the Colonial period, the Europeans had brought with them strict religious guidelines that they must live by, and in stark contrast and opposition to how the American Indian practiced their religion. The white man believed that he was superior to all of creation, and that he was to conquer and have dominion over the earth and all living things, whereas the Indian realized that he was only a part of Great Spirits creation, and thereby, he was compelled to live in harmony and balance with his Sacred Earth Mother, his environment, and all other living things.

Too often using his religion to justify his abuse, disrespect, and annihilation of the

American Indian, the Eurocentric white man, by deeming the Indians inferior and savages, he gave them ravaging diseases, such as cholera and smallpox, which killed millions of the native people, and to further eradicate the original inhabitants of Turtle Island (what the Indigenous called North America), the white man slaughtered the bison to near extinction, and not for food, but rather as a way to further eliminate the Indian, because the bison was the most important animal for the Indians' survival.

As a rule, the American Indians never killed more animals than what they needed for survival, but that was seldom the case with the Eurocentric whites, because they often killed for mere sport and fun, and…for trophies. Those acts the Indians felt were very dishonorable and disrespectful to their fellow spiritual family, as they considered all of creation sacred and part of their family; a very different way of looking at the world than that of the invading white man.

We have, no doubt, all heard the saying that "what goes around, comes around and you reap what you sow," and with that thought in mind, by the disrespectful and abusive actions of our European forefathers against the original inhabitants of this land, could those 'bitter seeds' that were planted back then still be instilled in many of the American males of today, and partly be a reason for their troubled and lost identity?

In many ways the American woman has surpassed the American man today. Perhaps it has happened because the typical woman has always been a multi-tasker: caretaker of the children, the household, finances, and…caretaker of the husband, whereas the husband who has been called the 'bread-winner,' typically has maintained only one job, be it that of a carpenter, mechanic, factory worker or whatever; but today many women also have jobs outside the home, and still they continue doing all the other jobs at home. Is it any wonder that she has surpassed the typical American male in so many ways? And the phrase: equal pay for equal work has almost become like a mantra for the modern woman, and rightfully so, but could this also be a factor for a division in the sexes, and also be a cause for many men to question their masculinity if a woman, who has previously been considered the weaker sex and a 'second-rate' citizen, suddenly finds herself equal to man? What can that potentially do to the psyche of many American males? Food for thought?

In order to get a thought or idea imbedded into one's mind, it is important to repeat it at various times, and one such thought worth considering for the American male to pay close attention to is: maintain a harmony and balance in one's personal life, with the environment and with all other living things, and…rid oneself of the pseudo-macho attitude that in order to be a "MAN," he must do only manly things, whatever that might be in his particular way of thinking.

One time a psychologist friend asked if I knew what a Corvette car represented to the typical American man, and I answered that I had no idea. The psychologist proceeded to tell me that the Corvette represented, metaphorically speaking, 'a penis extension.' And over the past few decades, if we observe how many men are driving big pickup trucks on the highways, but seldom ever use them for what they were intended, then could the big truck also represent 'a penis extension' for many American males that are seeking a way to embolden their masculinity? And what about the obsession with guns for many

American males today? Could that also be about them harboring the need for feeling more masculine; something to reinforce their male identity?

At this point, it is very important to see how fear plays a huge part with many American male's feeling the need for guns. Although many Americans like to think of us as a Christian nation, if we look more closely by our actions, 'fear' has become the 'god' of the masses. And as the Holy Bible says, "…by their fruits you will know them;" meaning, not by the words that come out of our mouths, but by our actions.

# Chapter 2

"For the love of money is the root of all evil." Although we have heard that statement many times in our lives, how often do we fathom its deeper meaning?

By the time of the American Revolution the new *'Americans'* had well established themselves in the New World, and there were many heroes and much greatness achieved in their early history…as one might judge greatness then and today. Yet, as a people, they were not satisfied with what they had, and they did not properly learn the important ways and lessons that the Indians were willing to teach about how to live in harmony and balance with all things.

As more of the early European relatives arrived on these shores, they demanded and selfishly took more of the Indians' land for themselves. Too often it was much more than what they needed, and soon this taking of the Indians' homeland became an obsession with the Europeans. They called it *'Manifest Destiny'*: obtaining all the land from the Atlantic to the Pacific Ocean, and…God ordained, but in reality it was brazen thievery, lust and greed. Once the new Americans obtained the 'Louisiana Purchase,' they were well on their way to controlling the North American continent from the Atlantic to the Pacific.

Just as good can spawn good, so greed can spawn greed. To live off the land and be thankful for its bounty was never enough for the early Europeans. An iron horse must be built to move them faster about. The horse of flesh and bones was no longer adequate for them. Yet all the while the horse still served the Indians well, and they needed or wanted nothing more, and  they maintained their pride as a race and were secure in their gender roles.  The Indians were called primitives and savages by the Europeans, and thus they must be eradicated…so it was declared. The Europeans decided that the Indians were heathens and not worthy of the land on which they lived, so the Europeans felt that they must rid themselves of the Indians and take their land. That was their rightful 'Destiny'…and thus they did.  In return for their land, they gave the Indians diseases, famines, death, and forever took away the way of life the Indians had proudly known for thousands of years.

As a nation, America quickly achieved "greatness"; more than the world had ever seen; but not without paying a costly price.  The seeds of greed and the lust for power and money had been rooted deeply now.  Those seeds would eventually contribute to a slow destruction of a nation from within.

"Before The Storm" Painting by Ed Breeding.

Some of the thoughts as to how the North American Indians may have felt during that time in history are wonderfully and eloquently expressed in the following poem by MARY ANN RUSSELL of Speedwell, Tennessee:

# BEFORE THE STORM

The old man climbed the mountain bare,

Seeking council of the Spirits there.

But the Old One seemed much older still,

As we watched him slowly descend the hill.

He left the village far behind,

And for days he sorrowed in his mind.

He sang the death chant day and night,

In mourning robes, though none had died.

Then when at last he chose to speak,

We saw a tear drop on his cheek.

He spoke of thunder 'ore the land,

Created by the human hand.

Of lightening streaking to and fro

From weapons we were yet to know.

Of rains that cause the river's flood,

But instead of rain the drops were blood.

A storm that raged with such ferocity

That our way of life would cease to be.

"But, Wise Old One, we fail to see,

How we so angered the Powers That Be.

Have we not quelled the human greed,

And taken only what we need?

Have we not lived in harmony

With every stream, and beast, and tree?"

"My young ones, you do not understand,

This storm has taken the shape of man.

And we'll find no mercy in his sight,

For instead of black, the clouds are WHITE!"

# Chapter 3

By the time of the American Civil War, most of the Indians' previous ways of life were no more. Although the White man still had much to learn about being a true man, as Creator had made him to be, he chose instead to put the Indians onto the reservations and colonize them; and in doing so, putting away those that possibly could have been his future 'salvation.'

Generally speaking, for people to feel comfortable or at ease with themselves, he or she must have a good gender-role-identity. By accepting nature as they found her, and co-existing in harmony with her, without feeling the need to transform Creator's handiwork, the American Indians maintained peace within themselves, with their Creator...and all living things.  In contrast, the White man, in his quest to conquer the complete continent, was not satisfied to live in harmony with the land and all living things.  Materialism was becoming, for many of the White men, their god.  The Pony Express, the railroad and the mining of gold and silver rapidly accelerated the White man's lust and greed for even more materialism.

Although the Indians saw the White man's way of life, they were not impressed with it. Instead, they abhorred and condemned it.  The buffalo, so long a mainstay for the Indians' means of survival, was brought to the point of extinction as the White man slaughtered them for sport and profit, leaving the carcasses to rot on the land.  In stark contrast, the Indian, learning from other animals' ways in nature, did not waste, but killed only what they could use, and thereby, the complete animal was made use of, including the bones for tools.

Another one of MARY ANN RUSSELL'S poems describes it perfectly:

"Why My Brother" Painting by Ed Breeding.

# WHY MY BROTHER

My brother, I do not understand,

You promised peace and gave your hand,

You took the grass, you gave me sand,

Why, my brother?

Because our worship was not the same,

And I called our God by a different name,

My religion you have called profane,

Why, my brother?

Sicknesses you brought from foreign shores,

And laid them kindly at my door,

My sons and daughters are no more,

Why, my brother?

The buffalo that roam our land,

Once as numerous as grains of sand,

I now can number on one hand,

Why, my brother?

I heard the sound of mighty guns,

As you killed the beasts for sport and fun,

And left them rotting in the sun,

Why, my brother?

In tattered robes the old ones came,

To shiver beside my impotent flame,

Their questions and mine are all the same,

Why, my brother?

My bones now feel the winter's chill

As I'm gazing down from atop the hill,

Tell me, tell me if you will,

Why, my brother?

As we take time to look back, many of us can respect and admire the Indians' past way of life.  But for the early settlers in America, the Indian was something that must often be annihilated.  And those that did survive were put onto reservations and into forced colonization. The children were taken from their homes and put into boarding schools and forced to learn the White man's way of life. Their hair, that was their pride and joy, was cut short, and they were forbidden to speak their native tongue.  Even some of our American Presidents were not exempt from that horrific atrocity.  President Andrew Jackson was instrumental in the removal of the Five Civilized Tribes from their southeastern homelands to reservations in Oklahoma territory, considered to be a vast wasteland.  Those tribes included the Cherokee, Chickasaws, Creeks, Choctaws, and Seminoles.

It is very important to understand that whenever a student kills his teacher, the student's chances of learning the important lessons that are before him…become very slim.  Earth Mother, the animals, and the American Indians could have been the new Americans' greatest teachers, but as we look back on that situation today, with the disrespect and abuse of our environment and other living things, we, as a nation still have not listened and learned.

If more attention and respect had been given to the Indians' way of life, and thereby incorporated into the White man's way of life, it is probable that a more peaceful way of life would exist for all of us in America today.  But that was not to be.  Too often the only thing we ever learn from history is…we don't learn from history. America today would be wise to study and learn a great lesson from 'THE RISE AND FALL OF

THE ROMAN EMPIRE,' and apply that lesson in our lives.  But have we? And the answer is a resounding "NO!"

At one time in history, Rome was considered the 'center of the universe,' and the Romans were the most powerful people on the planet, but when one thinks of Rome today, what does he think? Oh yeah, isn't that where the Pope lives… but what else?

This writer has been fortunate to have visited many foreign countries, and too often, whenever I have encountered American tourists there, by their ignorance and arrogance, they have been disrespectful of the people and country they were visiting, expecting them to always speak English, serve hamburgers, French fries, and such… globally earning us the deserved title of *"The Ugly American."*

Whether or not we choose to acknowledge it, today Americans are ridiculed and have become the butt of jokes with many foreign nationals. And although we may resent it, if we take the time to look at ourselves objectively, we may realize that we have 'earned' their dislike and wrath against us in so many ways.

Many years ago, when many in this country were blaming Japan and their imported vehicles for our economic woes, I wrote the following poem:

## RISE UP AMERICA

Rise up America while there's still time.

Don't just sit back and worry and whine.

Let's each figure out our part to play,

And whatever we do, let us not delay.

Rise up America while there's still light to see.

"Rise Up America" Painting by Ed Breeding.

.

Let's begin our jobs by getting down on our
knees.

Our country's in need of us now, more than
ever,

To do our part in pulling it back together.

Rise up America, let's clean up our show,

And stop blaming others for our economic woes.

Let's just be honest with ourselves above all,

Search our hearts and we'll see where we've lost
the ball.

Rise up America like the eagle with wings.

Do only your best for all living things.

Run the race while there's still time to win.

The Lord will honor those that begin.

# Chapter 4

The American Civil War: brother against brother, state against state, and White and Black Americans against each other. The Black skins like the Red skins were deemed inferior by the Whites on both sides of the Mason-Dixon-line. They must be suppressed if the Whites were to maintain a lifestyle to which they had grown accustomed. Perhaps we should all soul-search and ask ourselves this question: what good for humankind did that war achieve? We might say that it ended slavery, but has it? Really? With all the prejudice, racism, radicalism, and division going on in our country today, we may be setting ourselves up for another *"Civil War."*

Once more, another of MARY ANN RUSSELL'S poems gives us deep insight to the futility of war:

## THE WAR

We eagerly joined up without question or pause

To fight and to die for the glorious cause.

And proudly we wear the Confederate grey,

"Billy Yank, you'd best stay out of our way."

With exuberance we give the famed 'Rebel Yell,'

We're eighteen years old, and war sure is swell.

We're learning to march and learning to shoot,

I'm wearing a hole in my fine leather boots,

But, no matter, this war won't last very long,

Six months at the most and we'll be going home,

Waving banners of victory, all hearty and hale,

When you're eighteen years old war sure is
swell.

It seems like something is dreadfully wrong,

Who'd thought it would ever have lasted so
long?

Our boots are worn out, our horses are gone,

Those devils in blue just keep coming on.

Mournful sounds have replaced that infamous
yell,

Eighteen and a half and war sure is well. . .

My once splendid comrades are a piteous sight,

Scarecrows in uniform, they fall left and right.

I tell them the victory will be worth the pain,

But know in my heart they're dying in vain.

The last of my buddies lies where he fell,

# Nineteen going on ninety and WAR SURE IS HELL!

An established author and good friend of mine, whom I had first met in Wyoming, when I owned a cabin there, she, while reading the poem above, began crying. Her name was Eugenia Christensen, and her expressive emotions surprised both her husband and me, as she was not known to be overly sentimental, but nevertheless, Ann's poem did bring her to tears. And when I asked what she was reading in Ann's poem booklet, which I had let her look at, with a South Carolinian brogue, she said, *"The W-a-r!"*

She and her husband, Gardell were at that time living in South Carolina, where she had originally been from. She explained why the poem had brought tears to her eyes. "I have written and published a dozen or so books on Colonial America, and they are in many of our country's schools, and I have read almost everything that has ever been written on the Civil War, but until today, I have never read anything that has been so perfectly and briefly written about '*The War,*' until I read your cousin's profound and excellent poem."

As a veteran myself, and being associated with many war veterans, even doing a documentary film about war veterans called: SHATTERED REALITY, I am very aware of the horrors and futility of wars. But I had never heard anyone express so eloquently their feelings about war, until Eugenia shared her feelings that day at her home in South Carolina. Since we had become close friends when we first met in Wyoming, they had invited me to spend a week with them in their home in South Carolina.

Eugenia and Gardell were a highly-educated and well-traveled couple, and they exuded class, but without being 'stuffy.' I adored them both. And as I recall, they had first met in New York City when Gardell had been a curator of one of the museums there. He had told me of going on wild game hunts in Africa to get specimens for the museum where he was curator.

After Gardell's passing, Eugenia moved to Northern California to be close to family, and she and I continued to correspond for many years thereafter.

**********

After the American Civil War there was major reconstruction to be done, and soon the Industrial Revolution got into full swing. With the assembly-line process, and in particular the Henry Ford assembly-line process, the American male, though unknown to himself at the time, was beginning to perform like a machine in the workplace, as more and more men left the farms and other jobs to work  on assembly lines in automated factories.

Materialism was also beginning to get into full swing like never before, and as he gained in accumulating possessions, the American male began to lose some of his 'God-given' identity. He saw less need of the trees and wildlife around him in their natural state.  Instead, he saw how he could use them to increase his wealth.  The trees were cut for more railroads, more warehouses, more towns, and more houses.  The wildlife was killed at an alarming rate; but sadly, more than ever for sport and fun.

Although the Indians could have taught the American male about the price he must pay for abusing and raping the land, nevertheless, he chose to go forward to appease his own heart's desires.  The American male began to deal less and less with nature, and more and more with his machines.  He invented the automobile, the telephone, the air plane, the computer, and the machines in our workplace and homes, and much more was to follow.  In the towns he built churches to go to and worship his God, but the Indians maintained and worshipped their Creator in their hearts and in nature.  And although the American male continued to build more and larger churches for worship, in truth, he worshipped more the dollar.

# Chapter 5

The onset of World War II found a nation with the experience of World War I and a major depression behind it.  As American men went to fight in foreign lands, women at home were called upon to replace them in the Industrial work force.  And, the women did their jobs well.  They helped build the planes, spare parts, military clothing and sundry supplies.  They also began to reconstruct American Society.  When the soldiers returned, many of the women stayed on their jobs in factories.  That was a major turning point for the American men and women's role playing.  In no previous time in history had so many women done men's jobs, or worked beside men doing 'men's work.'     Underlying,   and   perhaps subconscious resentment was born and masculine pride was being lost for the American male.

In the early 1950's, more men went off to fight in the Korean Conflict, and in the meanwhile, television had been introduced into American homes.  Next to the automobile, perhaps no other invention has had such an impact on our society, as has the television.  In the beginning it seemed innocent enough with the family-oriented shows such as, *Leave it to Beaver, Ozzie and Harriett, The Lone Ranger, Father Knows Best*, and a host of others. Nevertheless, the new medium began to have a huge impact on how Americans thought, acted, and responded to one another. On the silver screen men were more frequently being portrayed wearing a suit and tie, working in offices, and although still being viewed as the 'head of the household,' nevertheless, seldom was he seen working in the ditches and fields, sweaty and with dirt on his hands, unless…he was one of the lower classes, or service workers. Whereas previously, the typical American male was identified by his grit and brawn, suddenly there had been a paradigm shift for him, and soon many men began drinking heavily, spending more time in activities with other men, and divorce was becoming more commonplace than ever before in the American household.

As the country moved on into the 60's, musical groups such as the Beatles, with their long hair and different dress code, would help ignite a cultural revolution. It appeared that as more rock-music groups emerged on the scene, our teenagers sought to emulate them, often to the point of absurdity. The writing was heavily 'written on the wall' that our youth was in dire need of role models, and so…they reached for anyone whom they felt was above them.

Not since World War II, with General Patton, Eisenhower and MacArthur, had Americans had their heroes. With no other heroes available on the world stage at that time, young Americans began idolizing and worshipping the latest rock musicians, with the Beatles and Elvis Presley as forerunners. A new heroic type emerged for the young American male, and that one was not found in mountains, or in our great American west, or in the trenches of Nazi Germany. Rather, they were seen in our living rooms on television screens. This 'hero' image was much less masculine than its earlier counterparts, as we had come to understand masculinity. That new image would soon begin to contribute to the gender-identity problem which would continue to plague the American male as time passed by. Unlike most women, he would not discuss with anyone how he was feeling inside, because he had been 'brainwashed' and conditioned to not show his feelings or be emotional, since those were 'feminine traits,' and only 'sissies' acted in such a manner, or so he had been led to believe.

Some American males began to partake in more sub-groups, and much less time in constructive unity with others. The inner-city riots from Detroit to Los Angeles would further add to the identity loss of more American males, with many street gangs being formed, allowing the male to attain a pseudo-masculine identity again, which previously had been alluding him. The very popular movie, *West Side Story,* showcased the power of street gangs in New York City. And then on the TV screens, more and more programs included excessive violence and killings, promiscuity, rape and offensive foul language. None of it was beneficial or helpful for anyone, but it became popular, and TV program ratings began to soar: money, money, and more money for the corporate world.

As American society progressed economically and materialistically, more and more of our youths' gender-identity problems accelerated, for both male and female. And as both parents began working outside the home to feed their insatiable desire for more materialistic 'things,' the children began searching elsewhere for love and attention, something seldom available from their working parents, and running away from home and living on the streets became a new way of life for many of our American teenagers.

# Chapter 6

In the 1960's the United States became embroiled in a bitter and 'un-winnable' war in Vietnam. This war helped to further plunge the American male into a deeper state of repression and regression.

Prior to the Vietnam War, most of our National heroes had been from the military. But no heroes emerged from Vietnam. Instead, our fighting men were ridiculed, accused, and rejected. At no other time in our history had the American male been so badly treated by their fellow Americans. The Vietnam veterans' feelings of despair and rejection caused many of them to retreat inward and escape into drugs, alcohol and suicide, like never before. And in our present time, there continues to be a daily average of 22 veteran suicides.

Negative repercussions from the Vietnam War are still being experienced by many of our veterans today that have not committed suicide, and it should cause us all to contemplate and consider what self-centered and selfish state of mind we American citizens were in, as a people, that would cause us to treat our hurt, broken, and wounded brothers, dads, and husbands as disrespectfully and dishonorably as we did after they returned home from that war. My documentary film: *Shattered Reality* features stories from men and women of that tragic war, and the film can now be viewed on YouTube.

However, it was not only the men who fought in Vietnam that encountered emotional, mental, and psychological problems. The men who stayed behind and retreated to Canada or

Mexico, justifiably so or not, they too have experienced emotional scars; scars from self-doubt, guilt, and uncertainties.

Below, THE DERELICT by Mary Ann Russell, again has a haunting and familiar ring to it:

## THE DERELICT

On a city park bench lay the grizzly old fellow,

On last week's edition, which served as a pillow.

His once fine tailored coat was reduced to a rag,

One hand clutched a bottle in a brown paper bag.

Dirty grease spots gave his trousers a shine,

I saw he was wearing a shoe of a kind.

The right shoe was black, the other one brown,

But they kept his bare feet off the cold winter
ground.

A rumpled fedora hid most of his face,

But on the part that was showing, there lingered
a trace

Of pride in the way of life he had known,

You could see the bench had not always been
home.

A clean cut to his jaw and an aristocrat's nose

Were plain when his face was relaxed in repose.

The friend I was visiting there in the city,

Just laughed when I spoke of the old man with
pity.

"Oh, that's Old Senator So-and So's brother,

They say in the war he was something or other;

A major, a sergeant, I'm really not sure,

But you can't always believe the stories you
hear.

The old man doesn't seem to be of sound mind,

He frequently partakes of the fruit of the vine.

And when he is drinking, the yarns he can spin,

Of his bravery in battles he says he was in.

He tells how he earned his medals of war,

Something about braving the enemy fire,

To retrieve a buddy who was wounded and
down,

Deposit him safely, then turning around

To return for another again and again,

Until he'd recovered the last of his men.

He boasts how a general once shook his hand,

And supposedly said, 'You're my kind of man.'

But you can see for yourself the state he is in,

And he's quite an embarrassment to family and
friends."

The humor she'd seen had escaped me
somehow,

As I tried to imagine his life up to now.

"Judge not," we are told, "lest ye be judged the
same,"

And I'm sure we're all guilty of playing the
game

Of hastily judging our fellowmen;

We ask where he's going before we know where
he's been.


*************


To contribute to the upheaval and turmoil going on inside so many of our men, the feminist movement with its demands for equality, especially in the workplace, may have contributed greatly to the "wounded" American male's low self-esteem.  Whereas before there were only men who worked side by side, now there were more women in comparable jobs, working alongside men. If a woman could do the same job as a man, that might cause some men to question their masculinity. That is not to say that the men were justified in their questioning of their masculinity; however, when one already has a poor self-image, it doesn't take much to push him further. As women competed more with men in the work place, a repressed animosity and resentment grew in many men toward those women. And as more women came into the work place in what had traditionally been men's jobs, some men found themselves in unemployment lines. Temporary escape for some of them was frequently found in drug use and alcohol. Where the American male had previously felt comfortable in his surroundings and in his male role, now he too often felt threatened by the women on his turf, but he would never talk about it, and that 'silence' could create a dangerous problem for his mental state, as time and history has shown.

Although those were the seedbeds for many of the American male's identity problems of today, perhaps the greater and more dangerous problems have been with the children of these men and women. They have been called "the latch-key children;" children who have been left at home with either a baby sitter, or likely as not, alone by themselves while the parent (s) work. This has been and still is one of our national tragedies. Most Christian and Secular psychologists unanimously agree that the basic personality of a person is formed from the time of birth up to seven or eight years of age. Therefore, whatever input goes into the child during that period will undoubtedly have a profound effect on their personality for the remainder of their lifetime.

In psychology a child has been called "an automatic repeating machine." Meaning, whatever it sees and/or hears it will attempt to imitate. Where most parents that have raised their children from birth have attempted to teach their children proper character traits and lessons of life, the 'latch key children' have oftentimes been shamelessly neglected by their biological parents or surrogates.

To replace the parents' role in teaching our youth, as the 70's came upon us, we found that a new parent for our youth had arrived. That new parent which had then become the most powerful National parent of the new generation was called the…TELEVISION. Parents quickly found the television to be the greatest baby-sitter they had ever had. It became the perfect pacifier for children of working parents. The TV programs appeared innocent enough in the 50's and 60's. But as we got into the 70's and at the ending of the Vietnam War, the TV began to take on a new and more powerful persona.

Many new factors were at play. TV had become the most powerful means of advertising the world had ever known. The negative and confusing issues of the Vietnam War were constantly present on TV screens. Human sexuality was constantly being more deeply explored and exhibited, and TV programmers gained more leniency in their ability to sell sex and drugs (pharmaceuticals) on TV. What was once taboo material to broadcast now became commonplace.

Although children were beginning to attain more material things than ever before, a great void was quickly developing in their lives.

Feelings of not being genuinely loved, along with the ever-constant absenteeism of the parents, caused many children to run away from home and live on the streets in some distant city, where promiscuity and disease ran rampant.

The sexual revolution was in full swing. Experimentation rose to the forefront, and with promiscuity came diseases of the body and the mind.   Parents no longer understood their children.   Children no longer understood their parents.   What the children wanted and needed most, the parents did not give: their time, their love, and…their understanding guidance.

Parents confronted with that problem often would reply that they gave their children everything that they never had when they were growing up. And sadly, that would be true. They gave their children material possessions, but not their time, love and guidance.

Whenever "unprepared children" began having children of their own, Pandora's box became fully opened, and thereby, all types of bad things popped out. Those new parents had not been properly taught the very important lessons of how best to live and interact in a healthy, respectable, and Spiritually-driven nation, and because of that situation, all types of new problems raised their ugly heads.

National government leaders, as well as CEO's of some of our largest corporations began thinking only of what was best for themselves, all the while saying that they were doing what was best for the people and the nation. And sadly, some of our nation's presidents have not been exempt from that selfish 'disease.' Our nations' leaders opened the door for the "ME GENERATION" to enter into, with horrific consequences for themselves and our country.

It soon became commonplace in America, for anyone to be considered successful, they must have accumulated great wealth, no matter how they obtained it. Whereas the original-Indigenous inhabitants of this country were considered great by how much they gave away, we considered greatness by how much wealth we obtained. Artists who may have created great works of art, but were not making lots of money from their profession were called *'Starving Artists,'* and thereby were not looked up to or admired for the great gifts they were giving to us, by means of their creations. The Biblical phrase, "The love of money is the root of all evil" was being acted out in almost every level of our society, and the results have been anything but good.

As the pre-eminent National leaders, as well as home leaders, the American Male was falling farther and farther away from what they had inherently known to be an honest and respectful human being, and perhaps saddest of all, they brought their companions and children along with them on that destructive path.

While working on a Mayan documentary film in Mexico, called REIGN OF THE JAGUAR, a Mayan elder said this: "It is imperative that mankind get in balance with materialism and spirituality, or they will self-destruct. There have been four previous humanities, more technologically advanced than we are today, and they self-destructed, and we are on that same path of self-destruction."

# Chapter 7

A new breed of American male was quickly emerging, a breed with no National heroes, and little National pride.  Many young men began to experience sexual and drug burnout.  More younger people than ever before lived on the streets, and the National suicide rate began reaching down lower into our youth.  The most suicides in the nation were not with the elderly, but with male youths from ages 15-25.  It would soon drop down to an even lower age.  What was happening to our youth in America?  Parents began asking the question, "What did I do wrong, and why is there so much rebellion in our children?" It was an important question to ask, but one seldom answered to anyone's satisfaction.

By the early 1980's, with the suicide rate climbing higher each year in our youth, their notes left behind told the reasons.  But by then a lifestyle based on materialism and self-gratification was such a deep-seated way of life for the parents that there seemed little chance of change.  With all the gloom and doom, surely the end of time was near.  And so, many people predicted such an event to soon be upon them.  With the muck-raking by some TV Evangelists, Christianity seemed to be reaching an all-time low, even though polls would tell us that there were more people than ever before attending churches in America.

How secure in his identity was the American male as we rushed into the 80's?  Homosexuality, since the dark ages, which had been a taboo subject to discuss, now came into the forefront in newspapers, magazines, TV programs and movies.  More and more young men and women were 'coming out of the closet' with their gender identity.  And possibly, greatly because of all their lives being repressed with who they really were, the homosexual male flagrantly and excessively began to express his 'sexual freedom' by becoming dangerously promiscuous, and soon an AIDS epidemic swept the country and the world.  Even though it was later learned that the virus came out of Africa, the homosexual American male was quickly stigmatized by the Reagan Administration, and because urgent medical attention was not put forth, thousands and thousands of young men were allowed to die horrific deaths across this country, while a vaccine in France had been discovered that could have altered the progression of the deadly virus.

Many National and local church leaders were quick to jump on the bandwagon with their condemnation of all homosexuals; calling them perverts, ungodly, and a legion of other vile names. With the church being the final bastion for help, hope, and understanding for homosexuals, quickly other organizations as well as parents, family, and friends joined the 'condemnation club.' Perhaps some of the most damage done by the church at that time was telling their congregation that homosexuality was a choice, and not a sexual identity. From that false statement and assumption, soon thousands of homosexual youths from a church background began committing suicide at a rate of three to one of heterosexual youths.

Even though the homosexual American male already had enough identity problems confronting him in society, putting his back up against the wall left him with only two choices…be strong enough to accept who he truly was as a homosexual person, or…commit suicide. And although it is seldom heard being discussed at any social gatherings, in retrospect, it is easy to see that some religious groups and sometimes family members can take responsibility for the majority of unnecessary suicides of homosexual people in this country, and perhaps abroad, and too often, justifying their actions on religious grounds.

Up to this point in our American history, whatever the typical heterosexual American male's problems had been with their identity, the homosexual male would have more than double the problems with his identity.

Later, three 'breakaway movies' would help awaken and educate the American populace to the life situations of "gay" men in America.

Those three films were: *Making Love, Longtime Companion,* and *Philadelphia.*

# Chapter 8

Four correctable faults possibly contribute to the greatest problems facing the American male today. Those four faults in our society are: embraced ignorance, lack of understanding, ambivalence, and prejudice. Without understanding and the prejudice that often accompanies it, how can we ever expect to offer help to anyone in need? The easiest thing for any of us to do is to criticize someone else for their (assumed) faults. And very often, constructive criticism, along with genuine love can be very helpful to the recipient. But to condemn, judge, or criticize without understanding can be, and often is, very hurtful and damaging to everyone involved. *"Until you've walked a mile in my shoes,"* applies here.

Even though most of our prejudices in society may come from a lack of understanding and compassion, nevertheless, we are also often brainwashed by the media, especially television, into believing what they want us to believe. Sadly, the media's motives are not to necessarily be truthful and honest with the viewer, as much as it is to present radical, sensationalistic view points, and thereby keep their ratings high. Any minority group, whether American Indian, homosexual, or those physically handicapped, knows the hurt and injustices so often done by media bias. With all that said, it is still the responsibility of each individual to study, learn, and thereby understand before we choose to condemn, judge, or ostracize anyone else. If, and when we do not do so, we are just as guilty, if not more so, than the person whom we are condemning. Pre-judices thrive best where there is 'embraced ignorance.' And one might ask what embraced ignorance is, and the simple answer is: whenever the truth and facts are presented for anyone and everyone to see, but some continue to hold on to their racism, prejudices, and wrong judgment and not accept the facts, then they have 'embraced' their ignorance, with the results oftentimes causing great anguish and harm to others, unnecessarily.

We all have problems in life, but it is how we choose to handle those problems that makes the differences in our lives; for better or worse.

# Chapter 9

With the 1980's far behind us, as a nation, we accelerated ever so rapidly into the year 2000. And then, what were some of the most prominent dilemmas facing the American male?  Four or five major problems readily come to mind:  Drug addiction, alcoholism, crime, homelessness, and prison incarcerations.

Hardly any newspaper across this nation could be read without finding an article about a local drug problem.  Just a few decades previously, drug problems in our children's schools were unheard of.  Today it is very commonplace.  How and why has that come to be?  In a nation that has achieved a level of greatness in which no other nation has ever come close, how could we have allowed such a plague to reach our young children?  To find the answer to that question, we should look at the lifestyles of the children's parents as a beginning point.  If we believe it to be true, the earlier mentioned statement, that a young child is an automatic repeating machine, then we can easily see that a child observing what his/her  parents and elders are doing has had a profound effect on what young children are getting involved in today.

The parents of our present-day children and their children were born during the onset of the hippie and yippie movement of the 60's; a time of 'free love', drug experimentation, and the 'me' generation.  With all of this perceived negative input behind us, is it any wonder that we have a young generation with drug and suicide problems beyond our comprehension?  We have become a society that does not like, nor does it choose to use and apply the words:   respect, discipline, and responsibility (RDR).  Yet those are the words, when applied to our lives, that can best help us with our problems today.

Perhaps one of the places where 'respect' is seldom shown is with our elderly people. Since too many disgruntled and unhappy parents are now living vicariously through their children, and giving to their children unearned, materialistic "things," teaching the children the importance of respecting the elderly is seldom ever taught. Except for being a free babysitter, too many grandparents today are considered expendable, or at best, placed somewhere out of sight in a senior citizens' organization. And when today's parents don't have discipline in their own lives, they are very poor examples of instilling discipline in their children. When today's parents and their children do not have respect and discipline as a guidepost in their own lives, then they become very poor candidates to take on any form of responsibility in any positive manner.

# Chapter 10

Modern man stands in need of his heroes. Besides the silver screen types such as John Wayne, the American male has had a long dry season. Not much in the way of National heroes has been had for many decades.

When America entered the 1990's, it became dramatically involved in the Persian Gulf War. Although our motives for involvement were questionable, possibly because of all the negative National emotions involved from the Vietnam War era, we as a nation, almost magically, became very 'pro-American soldier' once again. Yellow ribbons were hanging around town squares and homes across our country, plastic stickers were placed on vehicles saying, "We support our troops," but when asked how they

"Fires of Kuwait" Painting by Ed Breeding.

were supporting the troops, some simply answered, "well…can't you see the sticker on my car?"

Popular and sympathetic songs were written and played on the airwaves. Suddenly it seemed that a whole nation was behind its men and women in the Persian Gulf War. Again the American flag waved proudly all across our country.    And at this time Mary Ann Russell wrote another poem that can well describe a national sentiment:

## OLD GLORY

"Don't touch that flag," the old man said

To the insolent, unkempt young men,

"I've killed for her once, and you bet your boots,

I'd gladly do it again.

Now, you young whippersnappers have no idea

What that old banner represents.

It took me a while but finally I learned,

And I've loved her ever since.

We've put the 'old girl' through some mighty
hard times

And almost broken her will,

We came close to ripping her right down the middle

In the battle at Bunker Hill.

Her heartstrings were tugged by both Blue and Grey,

And she shed the tears of a mother,

Crying at night for the children she loves,

One as much as the other.

She's flown in lands with strange sounding names,

Iwo Jima and San Juan Hill,

On beaches like Palermo and Omaha,

Even Korea's Pork Chop Hill.

In Vietnam a few dissidents

Tried to drag her through the mire,

But when Khomeini reared his ugly head

'Old Glory' raised hers higher."

He told them the tale of 'Old Hickory'

And the battle of New Orleans,

Of McArthur, of Patton, and heroes unsung

Who visit sometimes in his dreams.

The youths saw their host was becoming tired,

As his head was beginning to bow,

And taking their leave, they looked at his flag

But saw she looked different somehow.

"Now, don't go molesting my flag," he said

To the unkempt, but humbled young men,

"I've killed for her once, and you get your boots,

I'd gladly do it again."


Perhaps more than anything else in recent times, the Persian Gulf War showed our nation's hunger for a hero. And although the war was short-lived, so was our hero's tenure. Nevertheless, we found one hero in the person of General Norman (The Bear) Schwarzkopf. A positive fire had once again been lit for an appropriate American male role model. After so many years of struggling to find his proper identity, the American male could now see a light at the end of the tunnel. And once again it was in our military where the hero appeared, but not in any ordinary man's, day to day life. In the general populace, a hero was nowhere to be found, unless it was a momentary hero that saved someone from drowning after an automobile accident, et cetera, quickly flashed on TV screens.

As the 20th Century drew to a close, America put more people behind bars than in any other time in our history, and it has no historical comparison. In the 1990's there was a 25% higher number increase in our prisons than in the 1980's, and nearly sixteen times as many as the average number added during the five decades prior to 1970.

Mental health issues and drug addiction are often at the forefront of men being incarcerated. So why does the U.S. have the highest rate of documented incarcerations in the world? In 2013 there were 716 incarcerations per 100,000 of the National population, and while the United States represents about 4.4 percent of the world's population, it houses around 22 percent of the world's prisoners. Rape is another major reason for men being imprisoned, but few people know that many of the rapes had little to do with men wanting sex, as much as it did about men exerting "power" over women.

So what is the reason for so many American males filling our prisons, jails, and detention centers? Could part of the answer possibly be that a large percentage of them are deeply troubled and struggling to find a balance and harmony in their male gender role? To enjoy using drugs and alcohol in a sensible moderation is one thing, but to allow them to completely control one's life is a completely different issue, and the latter is at the heart of why so many of American males are incarcerated.

This may be a good time to question why so many mass-murderers kill women. Although there is not just one simple answer, what if many of them want to kill women because, subconsciously, it may be the feminine side of their own nature that they can't acknowledge, and therefore, want to kill that part of themselves. It is time that we ask ourselves where a killer's hatred and anger originated, because only by getting a full understanding of a deadly issue, can it ever be resolved. With spousal abuse and murders of women at an all-time high in the USA, perhaps it's time we begin looking 'outside the box' for the answer.

It is a well-known fact that very few of our institutions help and encourage the American male to talk about and openly discuss personal and emotional issues that bother them, while at the same time, the female in our society typically hasn't any problem talking about issues on any subject whatsoever. For the sake of the American male's sanity, peace of mind, and being able to get involved and participate in a more humane and balanced way in society, perhaps it is time that they shed the 'old skin of the past,' which dictated that a man shouldn't cry, should never show weakness, not be emotional, and above all, never be his true self, but instead, always follow the dictates of the past that said what one must be like and do, in order to be 'a real man!' The pseudo-macho man's 'disease' can be healed by an understanding and application of the fact that all human beings, at the core of their identity, have both feminine and masculine traits, and maintaining a balance of those traits in our lives, whether male or female, gives us a more perfect being for our individual selves, as well as for society at large.

If we dare to look at the American divorce rate, we will find that after a divorce it is common for most men to get remarried within a year, but that is typically not the case with women. Why? Could it be that most women have maintained a group of female friends to communicate and share with, where men have not, and the women are not in a rush to remarry and take care of another man. By being multi-taskers for much of their lives, they can function quite well without a man in their life, but for the average American man, by typically being focused on only one thing in his life that is reinforcing his manhood, he is afraid and usually ill-prepared to go it alone in life.

This writer is well-aware that many people may take issue with the above statement, but nevertheless, it can be food for thought, and if more men should come to realize that it is okay to truly and openly be themselves, then perhaps the world could be much better for it. If they are able to forget about what society says that they must be like, but instead, cook if they feel so inclined, cry-share-be emotional-discuss sensitive issues, or whatever they feel compelled to be and do in order to be able to live with the only person they 'have to live with'  in their life...themselves. Then at that time, a "miracle" might possibly take place in their lives, for the very first time, what their inner voice wants them to be and not what societal pressures has dictated they should be.

# Chapter 11

## THE DREAM

Beyond the eyes of all I meet

On a busy New York City street,

Beyond the trying to survive,

And the struggle just to make a life,

I saw a dream.

In the heart of a most successful man,

Strolling California's golden sands,

Beyond the superficial aire

Of tranquility he presented there,

I saw a dream.

In the mind of a Texas oil tycoon,

Midst all concern of bust and boom,

Lurking there just out of sight,

Beyond the varnish of power and might,

I saw a dream.

He longs to leave all cares behind,

An ethereal contentment there to find,

That lends the soul a continual feast,

Where he can dwell with his God in peace,

And there he finds his dream.

"The Dream" Painting by Ed Breeding.

Mary Ann Russell wrote that poem for me to coincide with a painting which I had just done, called: THE DREAM. The painting was of a one-room cabin in the Rocky Mountains, with snow gently falling amidst snow-laden evergreens and distant snowcapped mountains. The painting was the result of a dream a friend had shared with me one day after he and I had returned from a skiing trip in Vail, Colorado. My friend ended up purchasing the original painting, and 200 Limited Edition Prints, signed and numbered were produced from the painting, and the prints, priced at fifty dollars each sold out in a very short time. Mary Ann's poem accompanied each print.

My very dear friend and cousin, MARY ANN RUSSELL died in the spring of 1990 from cancer at the too-young age of 49.  She still continues to be deeply missed by those who knew and loved her, as she was a very rare and priceless treasure.  In her poem:  THE DREAM, she beautifully illustrated the struggle and 'dream' that so many of the American males are still dealing with today.

"Mary Ann Russell".

***********

Although I previously knew very little of Billy Crystal, except that he was a fine comedian, I was drawn to see his movie: *The City Slickers*. And primarily because I had read that it was filmed in the American west, and having a love affair with the west since my youth, and now living here in New Mexico, I am tempted to see almost any film that includes good western landscapes.

Although Billy Crystal did have comedy in *The City Slickers*, the story also had a serious message, which I feel was quite well presented. The story deals with three American males who feel the strong need to get back to nature, out of the 'steel and concrete jungle,' and to do something which they feel a 'real man' would do. And so, they take a two-week vacation on a working cattle ranch in New Mexico. Their job on the ranch is to help 'cowboy' a herd of cattle up to Colorado. And though the three men were definitely 'City Slickers,' they proceed to learn some of the ways of our American west cowboys. In so doing, they each found a more secure male role image for themselves.

Although the story may seem to have a somewhat 'Pollyanic,' type of solution to a major problem that still face many men today, the film had merit in that it does address an issue which is paramount in many American males' minds.

Another glimmer of hope for the American male was in the form of a cover story in Newsweek Magazine on June 24, 1991, and it is still valid today.  The cover title was: WHAT DO MEN REALLY WANT? NOW THEY HAVE A MOVEMENT OF THEIR OWN.  In the article, one section stated, "…the movement looks inward.  It seeks to resolve the spiritual crisis of the American man, a sex that paradoxically dominates the prison population as overwhelmingly as it does the United States Senate….The Women's Movement had made tremendous strides in providing a place for women in the world… the Men's Movement is going to provide a place for men in the heart."

The article continued to talk about men beginning to understand the importance of learning from one another, and also the sad fact that some male 'friends' had shared nothing deeper together than a beer. Another notable quote from the article stated that the movement, "…is directed toward helping us become better human beings instead of better humans doing." Continuing, it said, "So men are victimized by nothing less that Industrial civilization, which has stolen the father from the home, alienated man from nature and forced him into a suit and tie so he can run the country…but they know what they are seeking. They are seeking communion with other men, an 'honoring' or a 'blessing', as it is called. This is the quality that was missing in their relationship with their fathers and what they have been seeking ever since, often from women. It is no accident that many men find their way to the men's movement after the breakup of a marriage, or long-term relationship. Love fails them because they expect women to heal the wounds of their boyhoods, and that can come only from other men."

That 'Men's Movement' appears to have gotten its momentum after the PBS special of Bill Moyer's 1990 documentary on the poet, Robert Bly. The show was called 'A Gathering of Men,' Since then, according to the Newsweek report, many professional and non-professional men, from college professors and computer salesmen to construction workers, are paying approximately $250.00 for a weekend retreat with other men. They leave their inhibitions behind and experience, among other things, the traditional Native American 'Sweat Lodge.' The article mentions that while in the Sweat Lodge, "There was a lot of crying, screaming, yelling, and gurgling sounds that came up."

Whether one believes or not that the American male has needs of such week-end retreats, there are many grim statistics which show that he is in great need of something. With our prisons over-filling and the drug abuse, spousal abuse, and alcohol and crime rates continuing to increase among males, something must be done soon or our better ways of life as we have known them in the past may never again be attained.

For the past decades we have been hearing the phrase, 'Male Bonding.' What does it mean? Are they just catchy words that can fit in nicely during conversation? Or is it something more relevant than that? Good psychology teaches us that before a man can relate at his best with a woman, he must first learn to relate and identify with his fellow man-male.  As we briefly look back into our American history, we may recall that young boys, from Colonial times until around World War II, were under the tutelage of either their father, or another male family member.  The male role model was well established then.  The proper 'bonding' was achieved at that time.  But by the late 40's and early 50's, as more fathers and older male family members went away from the home and the farm to work elsewhere, the young male children were left to be cared for by women.  By not having the male role model there consistently in the young boy's life, many a young boy began to develop an identity problem.

Often the word 'sissy' would be heard in describing a young boy whose mannerisms took on some of the ways of his female role models.  Later into the 50's and 60's the word 'queer' would be used in describing an effeminate male. And then that later blossomed into the common usage of the unspeakable word, 'homosexual or gay.' Along with this came a high percentage of homophobia in our society. Thankfully, now in our present day, only some Fundamentalist religious groups appear to have a monopoly on homophobia. It is very important to understand that human sexuality is complex, and it is not as simple as "me Tarzan, you Jane!" And whenever we choose to label someone in such a black and white way, then we can create problems for others, as well as for ourselves.

In order for the 'lost' American male to find his rightful place in society today, perhaps it is necessary for him to revert to a time in our history when he was more stable with his role identity, and then he can carefully study where we as a society have gone wrong in contributing to his feelings of inadequacies.  Only in knowing where someone has been, can we truly understand where he is coming from.

If we are ever to grasp control of the problems our youths are struggling with today, we must be willing to invest more time with them, especially in their first to seventh or eighth year of life.  We must also be willing to come to terms with the fact that if we continue to work for material gain rather than to give all the time which we are realistically capable of to our youth, then we can continue to expect identity problems, drug and alcohol abuse, and also an ever increasing suicide rate and incarcerations with our children.

For far too long the American male has been taught to suppress his feelings.  He's been told that he's not supposed to cry.  "It isn't manly."  Whereas women in our society have been known to share their emotions with other women and men, the American male has somehow been taught to repress his feeling and emotions, which in return has caused a legion of problems for the male and female.

If the American male is ever to be at peace with himself and his gender identity, he must learn to rid himself of the 'excess baggage' which he has allowed to accumulate in his psyche and on his shoulders for far too many years. It can be replaced with understanding as to how his Creator made him in perfection. It is very important to realize that our Creator chose to make a wide variety and range of personality types and traits, which are acceptable and good, and therefore not to be ashamed of, no matter what anyone might say. We must learn to 'un-tunnel vision' ourselves into a new way of thinking, whereby we can feel free to open up and truly share ourselves, as we really are, with other men and women, without the fears of condemnation and rejection. By doing so, we may learn that it is our individual differences that make us so uniquely wonderful, but not better, than other animals.  Therefore, we should not strive to be like anyone else, but instead, learn how to make the most of our uniqueness that Creator has given to us, and offer THANKS to Creator for being just who we are; nothing more, but nothing less.

In studying the nature of Creator, we learn that she/he is complete female and male.  Not just one gender. And when we delve deeper into who and what Creator says he/she is: "I am Spirit; worship me in Spirit and in truth." And where the Bible says that mankind is made in the image of God, doesn't it stand to reason that it means our "spirit" is made in the image of God? Nowhere in the Bible does it say that God is a physical woman or a man. If we are to respect, honor, and emulate our Creator, should it not behoove us to first see ourselves as a complete person first, instead of only thinking of ourselves as a limited male or female?

If we take a closer look at Jesus the Christ's life, although his Spirit was housed in a male body, he maintained a perfect balance of both male and female traits, a perfect Two-Spirit, and if one may immediately question what his feminine traits were, they were love, compassion, understanding, emotions, and empathy. Many times we limit ourselves unnecessarily because of our limited view of who we really are. Dare I say again…we are first and foremost a spiritual being who is merely having a physical experience in this dimension on earth, a dimension of existence which is known by many as 'MAYA-ILLUSION.'

In 1989 the Indigenous LGBT community in Winnipeg, Manitoba, Canada chose to adopt the term "Two-Spirit" from the Ojibwe language, wanting to be identified with their respective tribes, and thus, not be grouped with other races that use the term, "LGBT." They were seeking a way to remove themselves from a culture that emphasized sexuality over spirituality, and adopting the Two-Spirit term was the best answer for them, and so they took it and have applied it ever since.

To claim the role of a Two-Spirit, it is necessary to take up the *Spiritual* responsibility that the role traditionally had. That role includes prayer and a responsibility to be of service to the elders, youth, and mankind, and assist in the much needed balance of spirit.

Before contact with the first invading Europeans, most all of the North American

Indigenous societies acknowledged three to five gender roles, and they consisted of the male, female, Two-Spirit female, Two-Spirit male, and the transgendered. They believed that some people were born with the spirit of both genders, not unlike having two spirits in one body, and they honored that, for the Two-Spirits were highly revered, and families that had them were considered fortunate, because a person that was able to see the world through the eyes of both genders at the same time was a gift from the Great Spirit, our Creator. Oftentimes Two-Spirits held positions within their tribes that earned them great respect. Some would become Shamans, and others would become Mystics, Medicine men/women, Visionaries, and keepers of the tribes' oral traditions. The Two-Spirits were also associated with having a high intellect, many different artistic skills, and a great capacity for compassion and understanding.

But everything changed for the original inhabitants of Turtle Island (North America) when the Europeans arrived and began forcing their religion on the native people. Instead of seeing the gender diversity of the Indigenous people as a good and acceptable thing, the white Europeans judged and condemned them as heathens, savages and an abomination, and were determined to change them into their ways of believing, or…eliminate them, and the white Europeans did eliminate them by the millions and steal their sacred land; a holocaust that has not been taught in our schools, or seldom, if ever talked about today, but nevertheless, it did happen, and it has been said that Adolph Hitler got his holocaust idea from the early Europeans' treatment of the American Indian.

It is not very difficult to see from where the rotten seeds of discrimination, racism, sexism, and classism came from, and why they are still flourishing in the USA today. And it all goes back to the first White Europeans' feeling of superiority over all races, and they didn't stop from planting their rotten seeds just in all of the Americas, they also went on to India, Australia, and other parts of the world, thereby causing chaos and wars wherever they went. In our present day, White Nationalism with its rotten and ugly head has risen again in the USA, along with horrific and deadly results. And perhaps one of the saddest and most disgusting things about them is that so many of them call themselves "CHRISTIANS," dishonoring and disrespecting the true Christian.

If we will be so bold to begin wiping the slate clean, as a nation, of all of our errors, arrogance, disrespect, greed, and feelings of superiority, we may want to begin by realizing the fact that we are not "The America," but instead, only one country that is a part of "The Americas!" And that includes all of North, Central, and South AMERICA! It is fair to say we are The United States of America, but to think of us solely as "AMERICA," is incorrect.

With all of that past history behind us, is it any wonder that the "USA" male is still plagued with so many identity problems today. If we had a choice, it is fair to say, we may all want a simple solution for much of the problems the USA male faces today, and I will be so bold to say that the simplest answer lies in the ability of men to begin living in harmony and balance with their "TRUE" self, and unload the labels and identities that society has placed upon them, and also apply the act of living in harmony and balance with their environment and with all other living things…respectfully!

So…in conclusion, how does the USA male go about being content and at peace with himself, with others and all living things? Perhaps the answer lies in him first having 'communion' with himself and begin to learn who his individual and unique "self" is, and in doing so, respect and honor his true-self, and discard the labels that an out-of-balance society has said that he should be. And once again, Mary Ann Russell's poem leaves us all with something to ponder and think seriously about:

## **PLASTIC PEOPLE**

They've been Xeroxed every one,

Moving as in unison,

All of the same purpose, all the same kind,

All from the same assembly line;

Plastic people.

They leave for work by the morning sun,

Taking lunch from twelve 'till one,

Echoing phony people sounds,

Passing synthetic smiles around;

Plastic people.

Duplicates and reprints without names,

Their fears and anxieties all the same,

Moving mechanically to and fro,

Absently nodding yes and no;

Plastic people.

What odious machine has produced such beings?

These robots so devoid of feelings,

Hollow copies from the selfsame mold,

Where are their hearts, where are their souls?

Plastic people.

The "One percent:" corporations, political and some religious leaders have done an excellent job of attempting to make "robots" of us all, in order to have power and control over us, and by allowing that to happen in our lives, we have become angry, sad, lost, and always searching for a deeper meaning in our lives, forgetting the fact that we are first and foremost a Spiritual being, merely having a physical experience here on Planet earth in this 'vehicle' we call our body.

And it is so extremely important to understand the attributes of our spirit, which we possess. Again, those attributes are: love, peace, bliss, compassion, empathy, and understanding. Whenever we can stop identifying ourselves with our physical bodies, and understand that the "driver of our vehicle" is Spirit, then we may begin to experience what some would describe as miracles, taking place in our lives. When we are truly honest with ourselves, we find that it is oftentimes those rare people that have dared to be their individual and true self that we admire the most, and many times we may find them in the field of the arts, where society has given them 'carte blanche' to be "different." And as we all know, many of them become rich and famous for being THEMSELVES!

Not unlike the snake that sheds its old skin each year, and allows a new skin to grow and replace it, so the sad, troubled, confused, and angry USA male can also do the same…if he so chooses. We have all heard the definition of insanity: when someone continues to do things the same way every time, but expecting different results.

This book has focused on the issues and problems facing the USA male, but they are also issues and problems that many men all across the planet are dealing with, and males in this country do not have a monopoly on them. Let's wish all men and women on our Sacred Earth Mother bon voyage and Namaste!

Ed Breeding is a writer, painter, photographer, documentary filmmaker.  His letters have been published nine times in our nation's newspaper: USA Today.  His documentaries have been shown on PBS TV stations across the country, as well as National Film Festivals.  Some of his films can be viewed on YouTube and Amazon Prime, and all of his books are available on Amazon.  Ed lives in Las Cruces, New Mexico.

Other books by Ed Breeding:

THE BELT AND BEYOND

ABSAROKA AWAKENING

A JUST PEACE

MURDER ON THE WIND

DEATH BEFORE DYING

AWAKENED AND LIVING THEIR TRUTH

LIFE IS A JOURNEY TO HERE